Text by Rupert O. Matthews
CLB 1263
© 1985 Illustrations and text: Colour Library Books Ltd., Guildford, Surrey, England.
Display and text filmsetting by Acesetters Ltd., Richmond, Surrey, England.
Published 1985 by Crescent Books, distributed by Crown Publishers, Inc.
Printed in Spain.
ISBN 0 517 456273
h g f e d c b a

ENGLAND

Land of many Dreams

Text by
Rupert O. Matthews

COLOUR LIBRARY BOOKS

The low-lying mist spread itself out across the fields and meadows, pushing its fingers past the trees and through the hedgerows as the cows took their first mouthfuls of grass in the early morning. As the mist crept along the village street, past the pub and across the green, the church bells rang out breaking the silence. Slowly the village came to life, while across the valley a train rattled across the landscape and, in the distance, smoke from factory chimneys climbed into the sky. Another English day had dawned.

The image of the English land is dear to the hearts of the English people, something that is an essential part of them. This is how it should be, for it is the English people who have made the English landscape. For one and a half thousand years, English men and women have been changing the land. They have altered the land to suit themselves. They have cleared forests, drained swamps and built cities to make the scenery of today. They have made England.

The story of the English landscape, and how it became what it is now, goes back to the year 446, when the first Anglo-Saxon set foot in Britain. When Hengest, Horsa and their warriors came to the shores of Kent the land was in turmoil. The Romans had left and numerous petty kings had seized power and were fighting amongst themselves. The Saxons entered the service of one King, Vortigern, in order to fight his enemies, but trouble soon broke out. Vortigern argued with his foreign mercenaries and attacked them. But Hengist and his men struck back and overran most of Kent and Sussex. Finding themselves in possession of great stretches of fertile land, the warriors sent word home asking for help. The Great Invasion had begun.

The descent of the English upon Britain was not a concerted attack, but the movement of many small bands of settlers. It is to this fact that we owe the basic outlook of rural England. The Anglo-Saxons have not left much behind in the way of material objects. The odd brooch or sword may survive, but very few buildings. Yet the heritage of the Anglo-Saxons is beyond measure. The sites of villages, their names and even the idea of a village itself can be traced back to the earliest days of the invasion.

As the news of rich lands for the taking spread, families and their neighbours would load all their goods into ships and head for a new life. After crossing the treacherous North Sea, the settlers would unload their goods, cattle and swine and rest for a few days near the coast. They would then make their way up the river valleys in search of suitable land. In the fifth century Britain was a wild place. Bandits roamed the forests and barbaric warlords led their warriors across the countryside in search of plunder. Out of these conditions grew the village.

The settlers soon learnt that isolated farms were easy pickings for bandits, who would burst in and kill anyone who resisted. It was found that a collection of farms was far safer. At the same time the then rather primitive level of agriculture meant that many farms couldn't be grouped together as the land could not support them. These two conflicting pressures dictated the development of the village as the basic rural community of the English.

Though the village made the settlers safe from bandits, it also made them tempting targets for larger war bands eager for pillage and plunder. In an attempt to avoid this fate the early Anglo-Saxon settlers created one of the main features of modern English villages; they are rarely on a main road. The Great West Road, or A4, shows this tendency to perfection. Once beyond London, the motorist will pass through a number of market towns – Marlborough and Newbury, for example – which were built later and for other reasons, but not a single village. What he does see are dozens of signs such as 'Midgham ½', 'Wasing 3', or 'Overton 1'. The villagers' aim in this positioning was to hide the village from any army that was using the road, while at the same time being near enough to use the road themselves. Invading armies were unlikely to know the area, so a hidden village was a safe village. The small collection of wooden huts that made up an Anglo-Saxon village was hidden behind a wood, over a hill or in a dip. Anywhere, in fact, that was out of sight.

As life became more settled and banditry was suppressed by stern kings, the villages could afford to expand and become more permanent. The coming of Christianity had a further influence. Though churches generally came later, it was not long before the Christian festivals became central to village life. Christmas fell at a convenient time for a midwinter celebration, while Easter heralded the return of life to the land as well as to the Risen Lord. The churches that did exist in early England were usually quite small and were built either by the thegn, or lord, of the area or by monks. Understandably enough, most of these churches have long since vanished but a few survive. At Bradwell-juxta-Mare, in Essex, can be found a tiny church which dates back some 1,300 years. But though the vast majority of Anglo-Saxon churches have disappeared their memory still remains. Much later churches are often built on Anglo-Saxon sites and dedications to obscure saints with difficult names are sure signs of ancient churches.

Many churches have been built on the sites of ancient village crosses. Beautifully carved stone crosses were the centre for religious life of many villages before they could afford a church. These crosses were often erected on another Anglo-Saxon feature of modern villages: the green.

In the days when ravenous wolves roamed the forests, it was a good idea to have a large enclosure where domestic animals could graze and still be safe from predators. Often, this enclosure would contain a pond and be surrounded by the houses of the village. In time this convenient stretch of grass was used for games and fairs; the village green was born. Another important step made by the Anglo-Saxons was the brewing of barley into beer, and the construction of inns where it could be drunk.

So, long before William the Conqueror set foot in England, the native English had developed the traditional village. Their layout of Green, Church and Pub has persisted for over a thousand years. Without it, England would not be England.

It should not be thought that our Anglo-Saxon heritage in the village ends there, however. Many of the names

by which places are known date back to the dark days when farmers tried to avoid the roaming bands of warriors. Nearly all the place names in England originally meant something. It is often interesting to take the name of a local place and decipher its origins. Some, such as Beech Hill in Berkshire, have obvious meanings and are usually modern villages. Others refer to ancient words that have long since disappeared from the English language.

One of the most important of these is the -ing ending. This can usually be translated as 'followers of' or 'tribe of'. Hastings, for example, was settled by the followers of a lord called Haesta. Another very common ending is -ley, -ly or -leigh, all of which derive from the Anglo-Saxon word leah. This word meant a clearing in a forest, so a group of villages whose names end in -ley is a good indication that an area was once covered by dense forest. Likewise, any place name ending in -well can be taken to be the site of a spring. Not all name endings are so helpful. The suffix -stead derives from stede, which simply meant 'the place of'. Thus Polstead is 'the place of the pool' and Minstead is 'the place of mint'. Stoke, which is such an amazingly popular name throughout England, came from stoc which had an equally wide-ranging meaning: gateway.

Just as the Anglo-Saxons were getting their lifestyle sorted out, with a profusion of villages and a few market towns, the whole of society reeled under a sudden onslaught. Fierce, pagan barbarians threw themselves at the country. Farms, villages and towns were burnt to the ground while the air echoed to war songs that hadn't been heard for years. Land was laid waste and whole communities slaughtered. The Vikings had arrived.

When the Vikings arrived in England the land was divided into four great kingdoms: East Anglia, Northumbria (the land north of the Humber), Mercia (the Midlands) and Wessex (Southern England). Each of these kingdoms quarrelled and warred with the others, but the fury of the Vikings was unprecedented. The first Viking raids were carried out by small groups. Two or three longships would row upriver and fall upon an unprotected village. Anyone who resisted, or anyone whom the Norsemen could not use as a slave, was butchered, the village plundered and destroyed. Then the sea-raiders would leap aboard their ships and disappear before the local fyrd, or militia, could gather together. Clearly something had to be done.

But before anyone could do anything, the Great Host of

Vikings arrived. This time the Vikings did not come in two boats or even three, they came in hundreds of longships. In 865 they forced a treaty on the King of East Anglia and then moved north. By the close of 866 the barbaric Norsemen had pillaged deep into Northumbria and set up a puppet king to run the area for them. The savage invaders then turned south again and swept through Mercia, burning and looting as they went, until they returned to East Anglia. Here they killed the king, Edmund, and shared out the land between them. In the early 870s Guthrum, the Viking leader, turned on Mercia. His warriors smashed the military might of King Burgred, who fled to Rome, and enthroned their own king. The Great Host then invaded the only English kingdom left; Wessex. Within just ten years the majority of England had fallen to the invaders' swords.

King Alfred of Wessex had been just twenty-two years old when he became king and was still only twenty-eight when the Vikings attacked. The Norsemen, being pagans, swept into Wessex during Christmas and caught everyone by surprise. The land was pillaged and looted and Alfred had to flee into hiding. It was while he was on the run that Alfred is said to have burnt the cakes. It appeared as if the last Christian kingdom in England was lost, but Alfred has not been called 'The Great' for nothing. Within a year he had secretly collected a new army and then fell upon the Vikings at Edington in the West Country. With axe and sword the Saxons hacked into the pagans, taking revenge for the years of murder and pillage. Within hours it was all over and it was Guthrum's turn to run for his life.

Alfred was not fool enough to think that one defeat would drive the Vikings from his kingdom. He transformed the whole of Wessex into an armed camp. His introduction of defence in depth was to have an important effect on the English countryside up to the present day.

Right across his land Alfred built a system of fortresses. In each area he chose the most important village, or the most strategically sited, and ringed it with great earthworks and stout walls. The name given to these strongpoints was the Anglo-Saxon word for a large, fortified enclosure; *burh*. From this comes our modern word borough and the place name ending of -*bury*. It cannot be said that all the towns whose names end in - *bury* or -*borough* originated as one of Alfred's *burhs*, but many may well have done.

The *burh* served as a place of refuge for the people if the Vikings attacked. No village in Wessex was more than a day's walk from a royal *burh*. Cattle, pigs and provisions, together with any valuables, would be taken into a fortress to be safe from the heathen invaders. *Burhs* were not only a refuge, they were also part of an offensive strategy. The *burh* was expected to keep a permanent garrison of armed men, in case of surprise attack; it also had to arm the men of the surrounding countryside when they were needed for service with the king in another part of the country. All this was going to cost the *burh* a lot of money.

Alfred, with great foresight, realised that for the *burh* system to work his new towns had to be rich, and that meant stimulating industry and trade. Alfred, and his son, Edward the Elder, passed many laws to ensure that craftsmen and rich merchants lived in the *burhs*; laws with a modern ring to them. Tax concessions were granted and new businesses were charged especially low rents in an attempt to attract industry. Soon *burhs* became centres of trade as well. Markets were established in the new towns where all sorts of business could be carried on, from the selling of local pigs to the importation of fine silks. Laws were passed stating that any transaction of more than twenty silver pennies had to be carried out at a *burh* market. Another law brought about the formation of a group of men in each *burh* who would witness, on behalf of the king, any sale at the market. The royal guarantee that any deal struck at a *burh* market was going to be fair and honest attracted merchants in droves.

In building up a defensive network to repel the violent attacks of the Vikings, Alfred was laying the foundations for the market town system. Any modern map of southern England will show, at intervals of fifteen or twenty miles, towns from which roads radiate. These towns formed the backbone of England's medieval economy. Nearly all trade and business was carried out at the markets for centuries; without them England would have ground to a halt. Today, many of these actual markets still survive, but more often the old market town is now a shopping centre for the surrounding countryside.

As Edward the Elder, and his son, Athelstan, slowly pushed the Vikings back they recaptured first Mercia, then East Anglia and finally Northumbria. Whenever they took a new area of land, they would establish a royal *burh*. In this way the English way of life was saved from foreign domination and the market towns were established right across the country.

But though the threat of marauding Viking warriors, and all the horrors that went with it was gone, many Danes and Norwegians had settled in England. Much of northern and eastern England was settled by Scandinavians; indeed, Guthrum himself – the leader of the Great Host – was eventually baptised as a Christian and settled down in East Anglia. These people left a mark on the land that cannot be ignored.

Isolated farms and small villages had far more appeal to the new settlers than to the native Anglo-Saxons; a tendency that is still noticeable in what was once the Danelaw. The place names of an area will often reveal much about its Scandinavian past. Villages whose names end in -by began life as individual Viking farms, while thorp means an outlying settlement near a larger community. Other Scandinavian words survive in place names; words such as bekk meaning stream, melr meaning sand and thveit meaning forest clearing. Of equally long lasting effect was the different culture which the Vikings brought with them. Not surprisingly, the cultural lives of Yorkshire and Hampshire, for example, are markedly different.

The influx of Scandinavian settlers did not only have the effect of separating the country, it also had a unifying effect from which we all benefit today. Anglo-Saxon was a language with a highly complicated system of word endings which depended on clause and number. The Old Norse language had many words in common with Anglo-Saxon, but all the endings were different. So, though both languages may have had the same word for 'horse', any attempt at a sentence such as 'I tied a rope around two horses' would lead to endless confusion. Many linguists think that continued communication between Anglo-Saxon and Viking resulted in the dropping of nearly all word endings. The sense of modern English depends on the order of words in a sentence, as in 'Joe hit Fred'.

The enormous upheavals of the Viking invasions, and their great social effects, were only just being forgotten when storm clouds gathered across the Channel and another invasion began. In 1066 Harold Godwinson, the last of the Anglo-Saxon kings, was struck down beneath his dragon banner and England passed to the Normans.

The invaders brought many changes to the country, the most lasting of which resulted from their rather tenuous situation. As a numerically inferior group trying to impose its will upon a nation, the Normans needed protection. They found it in their castles. One of the first

things that William did upon landing in England, apart from falling over, was to build a castle. This action was to set the pattern for the rest of England. Where Alfred had built burhs to keep an invading army out, William built castles to keep one in.

The whole idea of castles was new to England. There had been fortified strongpoints and there had been the great halls of the nobles, but the two had never been combined. Castles, which performed both functions, were a symbol of the feudal system which the Normans brought from France. The knight, living in his fortified home and able to bring troops to battle, was the basis of a system which was to endure for centuries. The idea of a home being a castle has continued to have a strong influence on the English way of life even now, long after the feudal system has gone.

The first castles thrown up by the invaders were not particularly impressive. They generally consisted of the motte and bailey layout of earthworks and wooden stockades. The most noticeable feature of these earliest castles was the motte. This was the main defensive feature of the castle and consisted of a huge, earthen mound, topped by a tower. Many mottes survive to this day, though none has its wooden tower. At Windsor and Arundel the wooden tower has been replaced by a stone fortification which has survived the centuries. But these are the exceptions; by far the majority of the thousand or more motte and bailey castles now lie in ruins. The motte at Rhuddlan stands forgotten in a field some hundred yards from the impressive stone castle which supplanted it. Guarded only by a Department of the Environment sign, this motte is typical in that it could easily be mistaken for a natural rise in the ground. Nonetheless, the presence of a large mound at a castle is a sure sign that the structure dates back to the very earliest days of castles and that it has a long, and probably bloodstained, history.

While wood and earth mottes were quick and easy to build, it was not long before someone realised how easy it was to set fire to them or to knock them over. This discovery led to the next stage in castle building; the one which has left the greatest legacy in the English countryside.

The stoutly built, stone baronial castles began to appear during the twelfth century and continued to do so for more than three centuries. It is typical of the English that their greatest legacy from the Middle Ages cannot be neatly categorised or pigeonholed. A private castle could be anything from the turreted tower of Nunney to the vast, rambling structure at Berkeley. All that was needed was a licence from the king to crenellate and enough cash to pay for the stone and masons.

However, the different centuries and stages in history have imposed their mark on England's castles. In the twelfth century it was enough to have a wall of stone that would not burn down. Castles, or sections, which date from this time are characterised by square towers and angular walls. The mere sight of a twenty-foot-high wall and massive, bastioned towers was enough to deter raiders and bandits, but these castles had a weakness. A really enterprising attacker could send his men forward to hack away at the tower corners. Working with picks and shovels the assailants would prise stones loose and remove them. Finally, the whole corner would come crashing down and there would be a convenient gap in the wall through which the besiegers could pour. What was needed was a castle without any corners.

It was only about a hundred years before the medieval architects came up with an answer. Wherever a castle has a corner, they argued, build a round tower. The idea was soon adopted and from around 1250 onwards the erection of round, stone towers was begun. However, curved stones were far more expensive than square ones and so round towers were not as common as they might have been. Many lords, who had rebuilt their mottes with stone, could not afford to rebuild again. They contented themselves with adding round towers to the weakest spots of their castles. Even new castles suffered from lack of money. Bodiam was built in 1386, at the height of the round tower fashion, by Sir Edward Dalyngrugge, using money he had won by his valour in the French Wars. Despite this, only the four corners of the castle are protected by round towers; the gateway and other weak points have square towers.

The castles of England, be they magnificent, many-turreted citadels or mere humps in a field, are a legacy of the past, reminders of the days when knights in shining armour rode with flying banners across the land, intent on rebellion or loyalty, plunder or justice.

But war is not the only legacy of the turbulent Middle Ages. Between all their fighting and quarrelling, the kings and knights found time to endow the more peaceful pursuits, mainly the activities of the church. With the fear of eternal torment in Hell hanging over him, many a medieval knight, soldier or peasant sought to prove his virtue through good works. The good work which the Church encouraged was the giving of money and land to itself. This wealth was then utilised to pay for some of the most glorious architecture left to us.

Over the period the styles of church architecture changed dramatically. The style of a church can reveal not only when it was built, but how prosperous the region was at the time. The tiny Kent village of Barfreston, for example, has a splendid late-Norman church with some quite remarkable carving. At the time the village belonged to the de Port family who were wealthy enough to afford to build such a church. After this the village slipped into obscurity and the villagers could never afford to add to their church, the result being that the church has survived unaltered for almost a thousand years. By way of contrast, the splendid churches of East Anglia tell a very different story. For many years the region was typical of the rest of England, but towards the end of the Middle Ages all that changed. The sudden boom in wool prices brought prosperity to the region. With money to spend, the local landowners tore down the old churches and constructed new ones. Right across the counties of Suffolk and Norfolk can be seen the splendid towers of magnificent Perpendicular Gothic churches. It is difficult, in this area, to find a church that is more than six hundred years old, a sure sign of late medieval wealth.

As well as building parish churches, those hoping to save their souls could give to monasteries. Spread across the country was a network of these religious houses which has left a valuable and tangible record behind. These religious communities were the centres of learning in a world given over to the power of the sword. In these establishments histories were written and kept, ancient learning passed on and, most important of all, God and His Son were worshipped. At all hours of the day and night the monks and nuns filed into their churches to sing the praises of the Lord and to pray for salvation. It is important to bear in mind the attitude of medieval man to such monasteries. To him these foundations were essential. Peasants tilled the land to feed the nation and knights fought wars to protect the nation, but the monks prayed to God for the salvation of the nation and all mankind.

In such an atmosphere the monasteries were bound to flourish. For the greater glory of God, the wealthy orders built abbey churches of such beauty and splendour that the ordinary man was convinced of the power of God. Soaring spires and delicate tracery dominated the lives of the monks who toiled for the good of others and for God. But in 1539 the blow fell and the orders left England. Many monks and nuns had become lax in their observances and the people were turning against the corruption within the Catholic Church. Of more immediate importance was the fact that King Henry VIII had his eyes on the monasteries' wealth. He dissolved the orders and sent the monks packing. But the English countryside was left with a rich heritage of monastic churches.

The more remote of the abbeys, Rievaulx in Yorkshire being one, were plundered and left to fall into ruin. These ruins remain to this day and can be just as romantic and awe-inspiring as the great castle ruins. Other churches, however, were purchased from the King and turned into parish or cathedral churches. The parish church of Saint Mary at Tewkesbury was bought from the King for £400 and is one of the largest parish churches in the country. Though the great days of the monasteries in England are long gone, the heritage they have left behind is an integral part of the English countryside.

But while kings, barons and knights were building and destroying castles and churches, the ordinary peasant was getting on with his own way of life. This was, on the whole, remarkably similar to that of his Anglo-Saxon forebears. The annual routine of plough, sow, reap, breed and slaughter carried on, around the village focus of the green, church and inn complex, as before. Unlike the grand buildings of the romantic knights and learned monks, the wattle-and-daub homes of the villagers have rarely survived. At the same time the ordinary village of medieval England did little to enrich our heritage. The buildings have gone and the system of agriculture they used has long been defunct. That is not to say, however, that the medieval village has disappeared without trace.

Perhaps the most common sign left by the life of the peasant is the double bend of our modern country lanes. These sharp corners, which appear from nowhere for no apparent reason, have probably been the cause of more accidents and bad language than anything else on the roads. They are also a classic example of the 'historical leftover'; something that continues even though it is no longer of any use. It all has to do with wheat.

Seven centuries ago the pattern of agriculture was very different from that of today. The land surrounding a village was divided up into three great fields and each of these was split into a series of strips which were distributed amongst the villagers. In theory, this would divide each field into a neat series of strips each a furlong in length and an acre in area. Each great field, with its strips worked by individual peasants, would be planted with wheat one year, barley the next and left fallow the third. This ensured that each strip holder got his fair share and that the land was used sensibly. The neat pattern of strips, however, rarely existed. The boundaries were interrupted by marshy land, or rocks, or trees, or other natural obstacles. The result of these strips, and their inconsistencies, was that any traveller wishing to visit the village had to wend his way round all their edges and boundaries. The path that was beaten tended to be straight for a furlong, then turn at right angles to run along the top of a strip before turning another right angle and continuing on its way. When the strip system of agriculture broke up, the roads remained. They were used to mark the boundaries of fields and farms, so though it may have been sensible to straighten a road out, nobody bothered. After all, it wasn't too much trouble to turn a horse and cart, nor to drive it an extra hundred yards. It is only today, when the surfacing of roads has made their double bends a permanent feature, that the motor car has made their course such an inconvenience and danger.

Occasionally, a traveller will come across another mark left by the medieval villages upon the face of England. Scattered across the country are the remains of hundreds of 'lost villages': villages which have long since been deserted and abandoned by those who once lived there. Sometimes the indications of a lost village are all too clear. At Low Ham in Somerset a charming, medieval Gothic church stands all alone in an empty field, far from the nearest habitation. It is all that is left standing of a once prosperous community. But around it can be seen the signs of vanished houses. Mounds and ditches show the positions of cottages and streets. At Hound Tor on Dartmoor there is no church, but the house walls still stand clear of the grass-covered ground. Most of the vanished communities, however, are revealed only on old maps or in archaeologists' papers.

Why thriving villages should have vanished is a popular question and each village has its own answer. Hound Tor, for example, stands on some of the bleakest country in England. There can be little doubt that it was abandoned when life became too hard for the villagers. In eastern England a major cause of desertion was the spread of monasteries. When a pious landowner left a manor to a religious house it often meant hardship for the peasants. The new community needed all the available land to feed itself and threw all the existing tenants out of their homes in a very unchristianlike manner. Just such an abandoned village can be seen at Rufford in Nottinghamshire.

But perhaps the greatest cause of depopulation was the Black Death. In 1348, Death stalked the land with unparalleled ferocity. Nobody was safe from the hideous effects of the disease; old and young, rich and poor were carried to early graves. A man could rise healthy at dawn and be dead by dusk. To the medieval mind it seemed that God's judgement had fallen on this wicked world and no one could escape. Each summer the plague returned to kill those it had missed the year before. There was nowhere to run to because nowhere was safe. By the time the epidemics were over a third of all English people had died. It would take four centuries for England's population to equal that of 1347.

The effect that this terrible visitation wrought on England is almost without measure. Sometimes whole villages were wiped out, leaving no one to bury the dead. But more often the survivors of poor hill- or moor-villages would move to richer land to take over the holdings of plague victims, the villages they left behind adding to the list of villages lost in the plague years.

The horrific Black Death brought more changes to England than the poor wretches who lived through it could possibly have imagined. The drastic drop in population led to an equally drastic labour shortage. Peasants could take over larger holdings or demand higher wages, and there was little anyone could do about it. Over the next century or so the feudal system, introduced by the Normans at swordpoint, was destroyed by simple economic forces.

As the farmers (they could no longer be called peasants) grew increasingly prosperous they realised that wooden cotts and hovels simply weren't fit places in which to live. They wanted something better and were able to pay for it. The farmers looked around for the nearest source of building material, and used it. This practice has given a very distinct regionality to the English country cottage.

On the moors and amid the mountains there was no shortage of stones lying around waiting to be used. Unfortunately they were all odd and irregular shapes, not at all suitable for straight walls. But before long a special craft developed; that of rubble-stone building. A skilled workman could sort through a pile of rocks and find two that almost matched, then a third and so on until a wall was constructed. A generous helping of mortar kept it all in place and a distinct and lovely style had developed. Incidentally, this stone selecting technique reached its peak in the dry-stone walls of the hills.

On the more gently rolling hills stones were not to be found lying around for the taking, but there was an abundance of solid stone beneath the surface. This stone was quarried and produced neat, rectangular stone blocks for building neat, rectangular stone houses. The Cotswolds were at the heart of quarried stone building and within a few generations sturdy cottages had replaced the rickety and draughty cotts of the Middle Ages.

But in many parts of England there were no stones at all, whether quarried or found. Here, the art of timber building reached its highest expression. The timber-framed wattle-and-daub buildings so reminiscent of Tudor times began to take shape in the forest lands of the Midlands and Eastern England. The bare oak beams formed the framework of the building and were exposed in patterns that varied from district to district and persisted for centuries. This building style can be found in dozens of market towns from Shropshire to Essex, but is seen at its best in Little Moreton Hall in Cheshire.

In the Thames Basin, and other river lands, a building material was developed which would outreach all the others, yet it was not chosen because it was best, but because it was easy to work with, and was found locally. Broad river valleys have large deposits of clay, and when clay is moulded and fired it produces bricks. Across the valleys and estuaries brick cottages and halls, even brick castles, sprang up. The ubiquitous lump of clay was laid in patterns that were pleasing to the eye and strengthening for the structure. English, header, stretcher and Flemish bonds created charming patterns on a plain brick wall, while the use of different coloured bricks opened up possibilities as wide as human imagination. At Hampton Court Palace a criss-crossing of dark and light bricks, known as a diaper pattern, has produced walls of considerable beauty. It is unfortunate that modern construction methods and cavity walls have limited the bonding to the stretcher bond. This produces large estates at low cost, but has destroyed the chief beauty of brick as a building material.

If the average house of the average rural worker was undergoing a dramatic change at the end of the Medieval period, so too was that of the noble and wealthy. Indeed, it was not just a change in materials but of entire design concepts.

Throughout the centuries following the Norman Conquest, England had been racked by foreign attack and civil war. Any great house had to be as much a military fortress as a home. The bitter Wars of the Roses did not reach their bloody climax until 1485. England was not a safe place. But the firm rule of Henry VII and his son, Henry VIII, brought peace to the realm. The great earls and dukes were stripped of their private armies, brigands were ruthlessly hunted down and law and order became more than just ideals.

With no need to build military installations into their homes, rich people could afford to concentrate on comfort and luxury. The increasing prosperity of the lesser gentry, brought about by trade and a land boom, meant that there were plenty of people with money. As with the new rich in any age or country, the rising gentry of Tudor England wanted symbols of their new-found wealth. A hundred years earlier they would have built magnificent churches to announce their new position in life. But the wind of change was sweeping the land. The new Protestant faith was fast gaining ground and churches were not popular things to build. Instead, the wealthy built houses.

One of the earliest of these magnificent new homes can still be seen at Compton Wynyates in Warwickshire. Here, large windows have replaced the arrow slits and low, comfortable wings have taken the place of tall, stone walls. But the English are a notoriously conservative people and this charming country mansion is equipped with towers and battlements. Not that they would be any good in a siege; they are just there for effect.

Hampton Court Palace, like Compton Wynyates, was built around the courtyard plan and is equipped with towers and battlements. But the more ornate Palace better reveals a Tudor invention that often goes unnoticed; the brick chimney. During the days of knights and chivalry everybody, including kings and lords, made do with a hole in the roof to let the smoke out. Considering the size of some of the fires lit at banquets, this must have made for some very smoky rooms, not to mention the problem of incoming rain. By the late Medieval period some of the richer men were equipping their private apartments with stone fireplaces and chimneys. But these were both expensive and difficult to build.

The advent of brick as a popular building medium solved the problems. Smoke could be taken away by a cheap and efficient system. Brick chimneys became the latest thing. Those with new houses wanted to let everyone else know that they had the newest home comfort. Chimneys rapidly became more than just

chimneys. They were works of art. The large piles at Hampton Court reach into the sky in a bewildering variety of twisted shapes and patterns.

By the middle of the sixteenth century builders began to realise that they did not have to construct large houses round a courtyard, as they would a castle, nor did they have to include towers and battlements. The builders turned to the H-plan, which was to remain the basic layout of English country houses for centuries. In those days, these magnificent houses were surrounded by neat, formal gardens which have nearly all disappeared. It was not until much later that the vast, sweeping parklands made an appearance.

The castles, churches, cottages and houses of Medieval and Tudor England are obvious signs of the times to the passer-by; after all they are quite big. But there is another legacy from the period so taken for granted that most people miss it altogether. Vast areas of Eastern England, perhaps as much as 1,500 square miles, would be useless marshland were it not for the diligence of earlier Englishmen.

The peasants of medieval England may have been uneducated, but they were not stupid. They realised that fens and salt marshes would provide rich pasture and arable land if only they could get rid of the water. Many of the villages along the margins of marshes initiated reclamation projects. The organisation of these was generally pretty basic; each villager would be responsible for a length of dyke or ditch. Even so, the system worked well enough. These small-scale, private reclamation schemes can still be picked out on any map. They are characterised by the large number of small, irregular drainage channels winding across the land in curves and sharp corners.

The main drawback to the reclamation of the marshes by individual effort was that no large projects could be undertaken. This was left to the large, local landowners which, before the Reformation, meant the monasteries. The Somerset Levels were drained largely through the efforts of the monks of Glastonbury Abbey, while Christ Church, Canterbury, took a hand in the reclamation of Romney Marsh.

Despite all this effort on the part of individuals and rich landowners, there were still over a thousand square miles of fenland around the Wash at the close of the sixteenth century. That was when the Earl of Bedford decided to take a hand in the business. This enterprising landowner was fortunate in living when he did. King James I found England a rich and prosperous land after so many years in his bleak, northern kingdom of Scotland and he was determined to make it richer. Schemes to improve wasteland, be it moor or marsh, met with his approval and encouragement. Improvement and reclamation soon became fashionable on country estates, so it was not difficult for Bedford to persuade other men to put money into his scheme. By 1630 everything was ready and a Dutch engineer by the name of Vermuyden had been called in to help. But no sooner had work begun and the Old Bedford River cut, than the troubles which led to the Civil War interrupted work. Thirty years later the process was resumed until the Fens took on their present appearance.

Unfortunately, there was one small detail which nobody had thought of at the time. When peat dries out it shrinks. When the Fens were drained the land shrank, which meant that the ground level fell. Before long the land was below the level of the drains and ditches. To keep the land dry involved pumping water up into the streams. This was done by windmills in the eighteenth century, but electric pumps have now taken over.

When the drainage began the Fens were dotted with islands. These islands remained clear of the water because they were composed of different soils which resisted the marshes. When the drainage began and the peaty fenland soil shrank, the islands did not. They were left, literally, high and dry above the surrounding landscape. The most famous of these places is undoubtedly the Isle of Ely. It was here that Hereward the Wake defied William the Conqueror long after the latter's victory at Senlac. Today, the 'isle' is no more than a hill rising majestically above the flat landscape. The landscape from Cambridge to beyond Lincoln is entirely man-made. The dykes and ditches were artificially dug and even the contours of the land have been created by man.

Interestingly, while most people around the Wash were trying to convert water into land, others were doing the opposite. The Norfolk Broads are usually thought of as natural features, but are just as artificial as the fenland fields. Throughout the Medieval era peat was an important source of domestic heating in East Anglia. Peatcutters were kept busy digging as much of the black earth as they could. In doing so they created large pits, which filled with water and became the Broads. Over the centuries, the vast majority of these have silted up and only a few are left. These are now the target of much publicity and conservation effort, even though it was man who made them and nature which is trying to destroy them.

Another feature of the English countryside which has become a rallying point for conservationists in recent years is the hedgerow. A century ago the landscape of lowland England was one of small fields separated by dense hedges of hawthorn or bramble. Today, many farmers are grubbing up the hedges as the commercial demands of modern farming dictate the use of larger fields. The long, dense lines of hedges serve as shelter for many wild animals and are as much a part of the popular idea of England as afternoon tea. Yet the hedgerows as we know them today are a surprisingly new invention. Alfred the Great would have seen few during his campaigns against the Vikings and even Queen Elizabeth I would have been surprised at the sheer number of hedges in England today.

The truth is that the vast majority of hedgerows are less than three centuries old. Though this gives them a greater age than most of the nations on earth, it still makes them newcomers when set beside the village green or the monastic ruins.

The medieval system of farming allowed for very few hedges at all. The land around the village was divided into three great fields, each of which was further split into strips. The division of these strips was not attained by hedges, fences or anything else. There was simply a line of grassy, uncultivated land between the strips. Each peasant in the village would have a number of strips scattered around the three fields. This arrangement was based on the feudal system of land tenure in return for service. When the feudal system began to break down after the Black Death people began to question the open-field system. They reasoned that it would be far more sensible if a farmer had all his land lumped together in one block rather than spread out in tiny pockets.

From the fifteenth century onwards the process of enclosure spread across England. When a whole village agreed that enclosure was a good idea they would determine who should have what and then divide up the land. There can be little doubt that the changing economic pressures of the Tudor and Stuart years made enclosure good sense. But unless everybody in a village agreed it was difficult to enclose the land. By the mid-eighteenth century the need to enclose was becoming acute, but a lot of farmers would not agree to the enclosing of their land. So the landlords had to turn to Parliament to reform agriculture. As the law stood in

1760 an enclosure could be forced by Act of Parliament if the owners of most of the land agreed. By 1844 nearly 3,000 such Acts had been passed and most of England's farmland enclosed.

It was these enclosures which shaped the modern English scene of patchwork fields and hedges. Once a farmer had been allotted his land he had to put a barrier round it to prevent his animals from straying. In most parts of the country the easiest and cheapest form of boundary was a hedge.

Within a single season a village could be transformed. From having three large fields with no hedges it could become a patchwork of fields with literally miles of newly planted hedgerows.

The enclosure of English farmland ensured that agriculture remained a dynamic force in the country. While the rest of Europe clung to the peasant style of farming the English were building up the most efficient and enterprising system of agriculture in the world. The endless miles of hedgerows appeared to fill an economic need and they are now disappearing to fill another economic need.

But if the countryside was changing during the eighteenth century, the cities were becoming unrecognizable. The Industrial Revolution had begun.

In 1745 the rebel Charles Edward Stuart led an army of Highlanders down from the glens, then south into England. Stuart, or Bonnie Prince Charlie as he is more romantically known, was out to usurp the united crowns of England and Scotland, but his clansmen were more interested in the loot they could plunder from the English towns. Those towns were not very much different from the towns that Edward I had passed through on his way to hammer the Scots some four centuries earlier. They may have been slightly larger, but they were still rural market towns, just as they always had been. But a hundred and fifty years after the savage clansmen were brought to heel at Culloden, the towns of England had changed beyond recognition. Cities were growing in population and prosperity, civic buildings and slums rose with equal vigour and the nation was on the road to international greatness. It all began with coal and some enterprising businessmen.

The introduction of machinery to craft industries was to have an unexpectedly dramatic effect on the social life and landscape of England. Even as the Scottish raiders were being pushed back beyond the Borders, a new method of spinning cotton was being employed in Lancashire. The new machines made cotton yarn incredibly cheaply and hence the demand for cotton fabric increased. But the new spinning frames were huge machines; far too big to be of use to the cottage industry that cotton spinning had been until then. Enormous mills were built employing hundreds of workers and they became the centres for increasingly large towns. But of far greater significance than the increase in size was the change in character of the towns. They were now no longer an integral part of the countryside in which they existed. A cotton town relied on its surroundings for energy and food, nothing more. Its prosperity was not dependant on that of the region.

Textiles, particularly cotton, may have started the ball rolling, but the cause of industrialization was to be taken up by other men and products. In 1762 one Matthew Boulton constructed a large building where he could manufacture small metal goods. He called it his manufactory, which was soon shortened to factory, and a name and a concept were born. These early mills were built near to their power source, running water, which explains their emergence in the Lancashire hills. But a new form of energy was in the offing: coal.

In the early eighteenth century, iron was produced near to the minerals' sources, notably at Coalbrookdale in Shropshire. However, it was inevitable that the industry would spread to other regions; all that was needed was a method of transport. Horse and cart was obviously an inefficient method of transporting bulk cargoes; rivers were much better. In the 1750s, the Duke of Bridgewater was wrestling with the problem that no river ran from his coal mines to any industrial town. The Duke came across a millwright by the name of James Brindley and together they came up with the idea of building an artificial river to carry the coal. By 1759, England's first canal was open and running, transporting all manner of goods, but mainly cheap coal.

The centre to which the Duke chose to carry his cheap coal was then little more than a large village; Manchester. The town grew by leaps and bounds as more canals and more industries were built. Within three generations the village had become a dynamic city of 355,000 people. All across the country the picture was repeated; canals brought cheap transport which led to a booming industrial growth. By the close of the Napoleonic Wars, some 3,000 miles of canals snaked across England and the population was booming.

The total lack of fast and efficient transportation for people meant that everyone had to live within walking distance of where they worked. The concentration of factories in the towns led to staggeringly high densities of population. This concentration of humanity did not make for very hygienic conditions and slums were the inevitable result. Just as inevitable was the fact that those who could afford to, lived somewhere else.

The early days of the Industrial Revolution were the days of the spa and resort towns. Rich landowners could live on their estates, but rich factory owners could hardly be expected to live in their factories. Instead, they came to places like Bath and built for themselves cities of elegance and refinement. Bath (and other towns like it) was constructed as all city dwellers knew a city should be built if only the factories didn't keep getting in the way. The streets were planned as broad, elegant thoroughfares and parks, gardens and churches abounded. But the towns of Bath, Buxton and Scarborough were just too perfect. Though they were considered to be the pinnacle of achievement in their day, the very Industrial Revolution that created them would soon pass them by.

At about the same time that the first canal appeared, a new source of power began to replace the old water wheel. Thomas Newcomen had designed a machine which used steam to turn a wheel using the energy from a fire. Once the rotary action was achieved it could be used to power almost any machine. Unfortunately, Newcomen's 'fire engine' was very inefficient and was only used at coal mines, where coal was cheap enough to waste. In 1775 a Scot, James Watt, came up with a much better engine and took it to an Englishman for production. Matthew Boulton, who had already built his manufactory, took the idea up enthusiastically. Soon, cheap energy was added to cheap transport in the race for progress and prosperity.

The snowball effect of all this activity soon put the slow, sedate and labour-intensive canals under pressure. They were working to capacity and yet they still could not keep up with demand. More and faster transport was needed by the industries which canals had fathered; and it was needed quickly.

As so often in history, the crisis produced its own answer. As steam engines had increased the prosperity of industry, it was only natural that industry should spend time and money improving the steam engine. At the same time methods of producing iron and steel were advancing by leaps and bounds. On the day that Napoleon's regiments came out of the mist at Austerlitz, in 1805, both the problem and the answer were around in England. They met in the person of Richard Trevithick.

By the beginning of the nineteenth century the technology concerned with steam engines had improved far beyond the ideas of James Watt; it was now possible to build engines that were both small and powerful. Trevithick's idea was to put a steam engine on a set of wheels and let it power itself along. In 1829 George Stephenson unveiled his 'Rocket', which was far more efficient than Trevithick's machine, and started the boom in railways. 'Rockets' first ran on the Liverpool and Manchester Railway in 1830 and were an immediate success. They could transport goods faster and more efficiently than canals and the two northern towns boomed again.

Advances in steel making coincided with Stephenson's invention and made possible the long lines of rail track so vital for the growth of the railways. By 1840, 1,500 miles of track had already been laid and steam trains were powering their way from London to the industrial cities of the Midlands.

The railways had an unprecedented effect on trade and industry, both of which reached new heights of prosperity by the middle of the century. But if the railway barons thought that their new invention would restrict its impact to factories and mines, they were mistaken. The development of fast and cheap transport meant that people could now live a distance from their work. This freedom was further helped by the improvement of roads and the introduction of omnibuses. Within a few decades the slums of the eighteenth-century factory worker were quickly disappearing. Anyone who could afford to moved to the outskirts of the cities, where life was much more pleasant. Slums were disappearing, not so much because of the work of philanthropists, but because they were no longer an economic necessity.

The decline of the spa towns came at about the same time. The new, cheap transport meant that factory bosses and merchants could live near to their work and yet away from the less reputable parts of a city. Bath and Buxton slipped back into peaceful obscurity as the rich and famous deserted them forever. Only one original resort town remained a resort; Brighthelmstone. When the railway came to Brighton, as it is now called, the town was a declining resort like many others; the railway changed that as day excursions became a popular pursuit of Londoners. They flocked to Brighton in their thousands. In 1866 the famous West Pier was opened and the concept of the seaside holiday got into full swing.

'Dormitory towns' around the cities were another consequence of the railways. Suburbia, as we know it today, was quick to develop as the middle classes moved to towns and villages a short rail trip from the city centres.

By the close of the last century the landscapes of England were being influenced by a vast number of factors. The village was still the focus of country life as it had been for 1,500 years. Towns had sprung from the *burhs* of Alfred's day to become the bustling industrial complexes of Victorian England. The twentieth century had only added one impulse to the development of the England that we know today. It was not to come peacefully but in a storm of death, destruction and fire never before witnessed on these shores.

In September 1939, German tanks rumbled into Poland and war broke out between Britain and Germany. The most terrible aspect of modern warfare was that England could be attacked although no enemy touched our shores. In the summer of 1940 Hitler unleashed the Blitz on England. Savage dogfights broke out as Spitfire met Messerschmitt over the South Downs, and the stream of enemy planes seemed unending. By the time the conflict was all over unimaginable numbers of bombs had pounded English cities and nearly four million buildings had been destroyed.

Clearly the Government had to do something. What it did was to give itself new powers of compulsory purchase. Using these powers county and town councils quickly rebuilt town centres and put up housing. Unfortunately these projects too often bear the stamp of 'committee design'. The big building projects which could, in theory, have done so much for England's heritage have often turned out to be faceless, concrete jungles with no regional variety and little character.

This idea of council planning, where the local authority is meant to have the people's best interests at heart, is still a powerful force in the development of the English landscape even though no bombs have dropped for nearly four decades. Once government has such powers it is very difficult to persuade it to give them up.

Ever since the first Anglo-Saxon warrior waded ashore onto the Roman province of Britain the land has been developing. It has not grown through any great plan of government or of king, but because of ordinary men and women getting on with their own lives. Forests were cleared and marshes drained to provide more food, towns built to improve prosperity and houses built out of whatever was handy. But through all this muddle and confusion shines the essential English character. The lovingly-pulled pint of bitter may be far removed from the thundering railway train, but they are both part of England. Whatever England is today, it is because of our ancestors' hopes and dreams. Whatever England will be tomorrow, it will be because of ours.

Previous page: the rugged coastline of Cornwall is typified around Land's End. Clovelly (above) and Polperro (facing page) are two of the most picturesque villages in the southwest, lying in Devon and Cornwall respectively. Overleaf: (left) St Michael's Mount, Cornwall, which becomes an island at high tide and (right) Tintagel Castle, the legendary Cornish birthplace of King Arthur.

Above: twilight brings out the lights at Newquay, Cornwall's major coastal resort. **Facing page:** a replica Elizabethan galleon lies moored at Brixham Quay, Devon. **Overleaf:** (left) small boats aground in Newlyn Harbour, Cornwall, and (right) Kingswear from Dartmouth, Devon.

Above: a tranquil pub at Bickleigh on the River Exe in Devon. Facing page: the small Devon resort of Seaton, at the mouth of the Axe. Overleaf: (left) the columned Pump Room and Mediaeval Abbey in Bath, Avon, and (right) the interior of Exeter's fine cathedral.

Crossing the Avon in Bath, Avon, is the shop-lined Pulteney Bridge (above and overleaf, left), built in 1770. Facing page: the restored Roman Bath and magnificent Abbey of Bath. Overleaf right: the Early English tower of Wells Cathedral, together with the moat around the Bishop's Palace.

**Above: Cheddar Gorge, one of Somerset's finest sights, where water has carved beautiful caverns beneath the earth.
Facing page: Clifton Suspension Bridge in Bristol, designed by Brunel while still in his twenties. Overleaf: (left) the
modern Severn Bridge, Avon, and (right) the main street of Broadway, the show village of Hereford and Worcester.**

Gloucestershire is one of the most attractive counties in England, enfolding such tranquil villages as Bibury (above), Naunton (facing page) and Hidcote Bartrim (overleaf, right). Overleaf, left: Tewkesbury Abbey, also in Gloucestershire, witnessed much bloody fighting in 1471, when Edward IV defeated the Lancastrians during the Wars of the Roses.

Above: Broadway, Hereford and Worcester. Facing page: the arches of the Jacobean Market Hall frames the main street of Chipping Camden, Gloucestershire. Overleaf: (left) Blenheim Palace, Oxfordshire, the magnificent home of the Duke of Marlborough and (right) the Marquis of Bath's Longleat House, Wiltshire.

Above: the mill and Abbey tower at Tewkesbury. Facing page: Worcester Cathedral, which was begun in 1224 and finished, after numerous delays, in 1395. Overleaf: (left) a cottage at Hanley Castle and (right) Church Lane in Ledbury, both in Hereford and Worcester.

Wiltshire's Castle Combe (above), on the Bye Brook, is considered one of England's prettiest villages. Facing page: Gold Hill in Shaftesbury, Dorset. Overleaf: (left) Salisbury Cathedral, perhaps the finest example of Early English architecture in the world, and (right) Stonehenge, the ancient and mysterious megalithic structure on Salisbury Plain.

The fine coastal resort of Swanage (these pages) has some of the best sands in Dorset. Blown up by Cromwell's troops in 1646, the magnificent Corfe Castle (overleaf, left), Dorset, stands on the site of the infamous murder of King Edward by his step-mother in 978. Overleaf, right: Athelhampton House, near Dorchester.

The Dorset coast has some of the strangest and most romantic formations in the country.
Old Harry Rocks (facing page) are the shattered remnants of an ancient chalk headland,
while the aperture of Durdle Door (above and overleaf) stands on Man o'War Bay.

The Hampshire town of Lymington (these pages) is one of the more charming towns on this stretch of coast, but visitors usually just pass through on their way to Yarmouth (overleaf, left) on the Isle of Wight. Overleaf, right: Christchurch Priory, Hampshire, saved from destruction at the Reformation to become a parish church.

Sussex has some spectacular buildings and sights. Above: the Royal Pavilion, Brighton, was built for the Prince Regent in the late-18th century. Facing page: Bodiam Castle formed part of the defences against the French when constructed in 1385. Overleaf: (left) Eastbourne, one of the finest seaside resorts, has dramatic cliffs (right) nearby.

The Sussex town of Midhurst (above) is noted for its rural charm and fine pond. Most famous of all cliffs is surely Beachy Head (facing page), guarded by its lighthouse. Rye (overleaf) is part of the Cinque Ports organisation, though its ancient prosperity vanished as the sea retreated in the 16th century.

Though the oldest part of the present building dates to 1096, Canterbury Cathedral (above) dates back to St Augustine's mission of 597. Facing page: The Pantiles in Royal Tunbridge Wells, (overleaf, left) the Inner Harbour of Ramsgate and (overleaf, right) Scotney Castle, all in Kent.

The Tudor brick mansion of Sutton Place (above) was once the home of J. Paul Getty and stands just outside Guildford. The cobbled High Street (facing page) of Guildford itself is dominated by the large, gilded clock of the Guildhall.

The 163-foot-tall Chinese Pagoda (above) is just one of Kew Gardens' peculiar structures. Facing page: the Clock Court of Hampton Court Palace, perhaps the most complete Tudor palace in the country. Overleaf: (left) Epsom Racecourse and (right) the Thames at Richmond, both in Surrey.

As capital of the nation, London has many fine and historic buildings, including the
Houses of Parliament (facing page) and Buckingham Palace (overleaf, right), as well as a
touch of class, as (overleaf, left) in Rotten Row, Hyde Park. Above: Waterloo Bridge.

The massive edifice of Windsor Castle (these pages) dates back to the days of William the Conqueror, though it has taken centuries of building to create the present skyline. Of older ancestry is Hambleden Mill (overleaf, left), Buckinghamshire, which was founded in Saxon times. Overleaf, right: the fine brick and flint church tower and 18th century bridge of Henley-on-Thames.

Above: pleasure boats move upstream on the Thames through Goring Lock. Further west, at Oxford, punting is one of the more popular water sports, as shown (overleaf, left) at Magdalen College. Facing page: the gardens of Christ Church and (overleaf, right) the square tower of Merton College from Christ Church Meadows.

The charming buildings of Lavenham, Suffolk, date back to the days when this was a prosperous wool town in the late-mediaeval period: (above) the Swan Hotel and (facing page) Water Street. Overleaf: (left) the green at Finchingfield, Essex, and (right) the war memorial at Cavendish, Suffolk.

Above: the magnificent Jacobean mansion of Blickling Hall, Norfolk, begun in 1616 for Sir Henry Hobart. Facing page: the River Thurne at Potter Heigham, Norfolk. Overleaf: two of the more famous Cambridge colleges; (left) St John's and (right) King's College with its chapel.

Above: Houghton Mill on the River Ouse, Cambridgeshire. Facing page: the cobbled Steep Hill of Lincoln which leads up to the cathedral. Overleaf: (left) the spa of Matlock Bath on the Derwent River and (right) Chatsworth House, the 17th-century home of the Dukes of Devonshire, both in Derbyshire.

The great homes of Warwickshire are among the most charming and least pretentious in the country. Packwood House (above) is a Tudor mansion with later additions, while Compton Wynyates (facing page) dates from 1480. Overleaf: two views of Stratford-on-Avon: (left) the Royal Shakespeare Theatre and (right) Holy Trinity Church, where the Bard lies buried.

Above: Welford-on-Avon, one of the prettiest villages in Warwickshire. Facing page: the cottage in Shottery, Warwickshire, where William Shakespeare is said to have courted Anne Hathaway. Overleaf: Chester has its origins in an important Roman city, known as Deva, of which much remains to be seen.

Liverpool contains several notable buildings, including the starkly modern Roman Catholic Cathedral, (above) the high altar, and the Royal Liver Building (facing page). Overleaf: (left) the town hall of the industrial Yorkshire town of Bradford and (right) Blackpool's Tower and beach, the favoured holiday resort of the Northwest.

The Lake District, with its unique blend of lakes and mountains, is one of the loveliest regions of England; (above) Crummock Water and (facing page) Bowness on Windermere. Overleaf: (left) Whitby, North Yorkshire, and (right) the floodlit towers of York Minster rise above their ancient city.

Above: a view of Whitby Harbour from the steps leading up to Whitby Abbey. Facing page: the picturesque Shambles, in the heart of York. Overleaf: (left) the iron Tyne Bridge and gaily painted Swing Bridge, Newcastle-upon-Tyne and (right) the romantic, mist-shrouded towers of Durham Cathedral.

INDEX